AMENDMENTS TO THE UNITED STATES CONSTITUTION
THE BILL OF RIGHTS

THE RIGHT TO BEAR ARMS

LARRY GERBER

THE SECOND AMENDMENT

rosen publishing's
rosen central®

New York

Published in 2011 by The Rosen Publishing Group, Inc.
29 East 21st Street, New York, NY 10010

First Edition

Library of Congress Cataloging-in-Publication Data

Gerber, Larry, 1946–
The Second Amendment : the right to bear arms / Larry Gerber. — 1st ed.
    p. cm. — (Amendments to the United States Constitution : the Bill of Rights)
Includes bibliographical references and index.
ISBN 978-1-4488-1253-0 (library binding)
ISBN 978-1-4488-2303-1 (pbk.)
ISBN 978-1-4488-2317-8 (6-pack)
1. Firearms—Law and legislation—United States—Juvenile literature. 2. United States.
Constitution. 2nd Amendment—Juvenile literature. I. Title.
KF3941.G47 2011
344.7305'33—dc22

                                                                              2010015854

Manufactured in the United States of America

CPSIA Compliance Information: Batch #W11YA: For further information, contact Rosen Publishing, New York, New York, at 1-800-237-9932.

On the cover: Left: A man shoots a Glock pistol at the DFW Gun Range and Training Center in Dallas, Texas. Right: A demonstrator displays placards supporting a case on bearing arms in front of the Supreme Court in Washington, D.C.

CONTENTS

PROTECT YOUR FAMILY,
CHILDREN AND COMMUNITY

GET GUNS OFF THE STREETS

INTRODUCTION

Some people believe guns are so dangerous that they should be banned. Others believe that guns are the best protection against criminals. In June 2008, the U.S. Supreme Court—the highest court in the United States—stepped into the argument.

The case was called *District of Columbia v. Heller*. The Supreme Court ruled that people could keep guns for self-defense. The decision was close. Five of the justices ruled in favor of a man who wanted to keep a pistol at home; four voted against. It was the most important ruling on gun rights since the Second Amendment was adopted in 1791 as part of our Bill of Rights.

A San Francisco police officer introduces a campaign against illegal firearms on June 27, 2008. Opponents of gun control sued the city, claiming its laws violate the Second Amendment.

The Second Amendment to the U.S. Constitution is only twenty-seven words long, but there are fierce arguments about exactly what those words mean. The amendment says:

> A well-regulated militia being necessary to the security of a free State, the right of the people to keep and bear arms shall not be infringed.

Does the Second Amendment mean that cities and states can't pass gun laws? Does it mean that schools can't have rules against guns in class? Is it OK for people who might harm others to have dangerous weapons? These are just a few of the questions people are debating.

Those who favor strict gun laws point out that firearms kill innocent people, sometimes by accident, sometimes not. They often stress the phrase "well-regulated militia" in their arguments. According to this interpretation, the right to own guns applies to defense forces like the National Guard but not necessarily to individual citizens. Others stress the second part of the amendment: "the right of the people to keep and bear arms shall not be infringed." They believe that private citizens have the right to own weapons, and the amendment says the government can't take away that right.

Guns were important in early America. When the colonists got fed up with British rule, they brought their muskets to the war for independence. Few questioned the right of every citizen to have a firearm.

Over time, America changed. By the twentieth century, guns had become more efficient and more deadly. Crime became more common. Laws were made that restricted the sale and possession of guns.

Many people object to these laws. Those who oppose gun control believe that law-abiding citizens should be allowed to have guns to protect themselves. They also say that criminals don't pay attention to gun control laws anyway.

The Supreme Court's 2008 decision ended a ban on personal handguns in the District of Columbia. It didn't change gun laws in other cities and states, and it didn't end disputes about those laws. However, it did set the stage for new arguments in the debate over the Second Amendment.

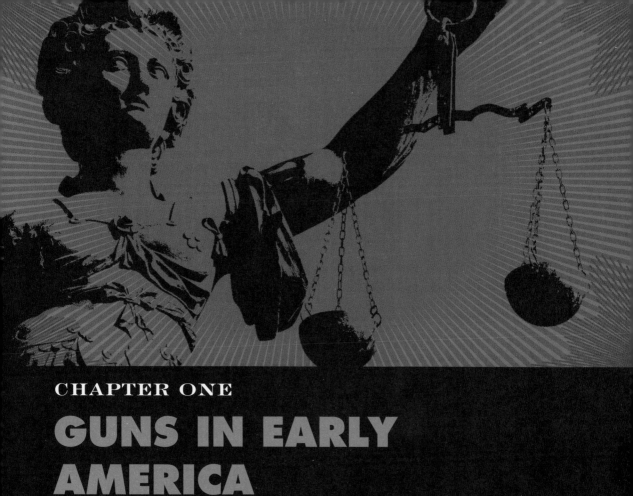

CHAPTER ONE

GUNS IN EARLY AMERICA

When the first English colonists came to America, they brought guns. Firearms were tools of everyday life in many parts of the new colonies, especially on the frontier. The settlers used muskets and primitive shotguns to hunt. Deer, turkey, and other game animals were an important source of food. The settlers also used their firearms against the Native Americans. When the first colonists arrived, many of the Indian tribes were friendly. They helped the newcomers through bad winters when food was scarce. The tradition of Thanksgiving recalls the early friendship between the settlers and the original American people. However, as more and more Europeans came

Settlers in early America used their guns for hunting and for fighting Native Americans. These Pilgrims in New England are shown walking to church with their firearms.

to the New World, they built farms on land that had belonged to the tribes. They killed or drove away the game that the Indians needed for food. When the Indians fought back, they were defeated by the colonists' more powerful weapons.

Early America had no police. If community leaders learned that a criminal was on the loose, they would raise a "hue and cry." This meant that they would sound an alarm for all citizens to help find and arrest the fugitive. To carry out their duty, citizens were expected to supply their own weapons.

Many of the early gun laws in America were not about restricting weapons. Instead, they actually required citizens to have weapons. In some colonies, men had to carry their muskets to church, where they could be seen and noted by the church elders. These laws were passed because community leaders feared an Indian attack or a slave rebellion and wanted to make sure that everyone who could fight was armed. Some colonial governments even provided muskets and ammunition for men who couldn't afford to buy their own.

Common Law, Customs, and Traditions

Settlers from England brought English laws, customs, and traditions to the New World. Even though the colonists would eventually declare independence from England, English laws and customs influenced the U.S. Constitution and the Bill of Rights, including the Second Amendment.

Some of those customs and traditions were thousands of years old, existing long before England was a country. Citizens of Athens formed the first democratic city-state more than 2,500 years ago. In times of war, every free able-bodied Athenian man was supposed to bring

his spear and shield to fight in the army. Ancient Rome had a similar custom. The German tribes who settled England after the fall of Rome were societies of warriors. Every man was expected to have weapons and know how to use them.

The Founding Fathers signed the Constitution in 1787. They believed that free citizens needed arms for protection from oppressive rulers and armies.

During the Middle Ages, warfare was an activity mostly for nobles, who had the money to buy armor and horses and the time to practice fighting with a sword and lance. During the 1500s and 1600s, however, inventors developed more efficient firearms. These guns made it possible for common soldiers with a little training to overcome knights on horseback. More and more people learned how to use firearms during this time, which became known as the Gunpowder Revolution. Armies grew larger and more powerful.

About the same time, Europeans were fighting wars over religion. Kings and rulers often tried to force their own form of worship on their subjects. In doing so, they used their armies not only to battle foreign enemies but also to subdue their own people. Civil war in England had major effects on the way its people used and thought about guns. When English colonists came to America, they brought both knowledge of guns and a mistrust of standing armies.

The men who wrote the U.S. Constitution and the Bill of Rights were well aware of English history and its laws, traditions, and customs. Most of them believed that it was not only a right or a privilege to keep and bear arms in order to protect their communities, but it was also every citizen's duty. They felt that the best way to guard against oppression by kings and dictators was for all citizens to be armed.

It is important to remember, however, that many people in colonial America were not citizens. Native Americans and slaves did not enjoy the rights of citizens. In fact, many of the first American gun control laws were meant to keep firearms out of the hands of Indians and slaves. Colonial governments were afraid of what might happen if they were allowed to have modern weapons.

The English Civil War and the English Bill of Rights

Between 1642 and 1651, England was torn by a civil war. The forces of Oliver Cromwell, an English politician and military leader, battled the forces of King Charles I. Cromwell's followers included many Protestants who thought Charles was too sympathetic to Catholicism. Charles claimed a divine right to rule as he pleased. Cromwell's followers wanted Parliament, whose members were elected, to have a bigger say in government.

Cromwell and Parliament organized a new type of army. Its men were regularly paid, well fed, and disciplined. Many of them were musketeers, infantry soldiers equipped with muskets. They defeated the king's forces. Cromwell imposed martial law, suspending many traditional rights and customs that English citizens had once enjoyed. He dissolved Parliament and ruled as a dictator. His new army gained a reputation for mistreating civilians. After Cromwell died, Parliament and a new king were restored. In 1689, Parliament drew up an English Bill of Rights. Among other things, it said rulers could not keep an army in England during peacetime.

During the English Civil War, many English people learned how to handle firearms. As we can see from the English Bill of Rights, they also came to mistrust armies directed by a powerful ruler. Sir William Blackstone, a famous legal scholar, later organized and wrote down a list of England's common-law rights. He included the individual's right to bear arms "for self-preservation and defense."

Colonial Militias

"Militia" is a word with several meanings. It comes from a Latin word for "soldier" and usually refers to a group of citizens who are prepared to protect their community in times of emergency. When they aren't needed for service, militia members have normal jobs in civilian life. The word "militia" can also refer to the entire body of citizens—everyone who could possibly be called into service, whether or not they actually are. In England's American colonies, all able-bodied men between sixteen and sixty years of age were members of the local militia. They had to attend military training at specified times. They were usually required to bring their own guns.

At this time, most militia members owned flintlock muskets. These guns were loaded by pouring a measure of powder down the barrel, then pushing in a lead ball and a piece of cloth stuffing to keep everything in place. The load was tamped down with a ramrod. Next, a pinch of powder was poured into the flash pan near the trigger. Then the soldier cocked the hammer, which held a small piece of flint. When he pulled the trigger, the hammer would slam down, the flint would strike a spark into the flash pan, and the musket would fire.

It took a lot of practice for a militiaman with a musket to be able to fire more than one or two shots per minute. It was important to fire as quickly as possible because muskets weren't very accurate. It was difficult to hit a man-sized target beyond 150 to 300 feet (46 to 92 meters) away. Armies tried to make up for this by shooting as often as they could.

A few militiamen had rifles, which were more accurate but took even longer to load. Rifles have spiral grooves cut inside the barrel. These grooves cause the bullet to spin, making it easier to hit targets at a greater distance.

America's war for independence from England began on April 19, 1775, when English soldiers on their way to seize colonists' arms and ammunition exchanged fire with Massachusetts militiamen.

Colonial militia units were called out mostly to fight Indians. Militias also battled the forces of Spain and France, who had possessions in North America. There were several bitter conflicts between English colonists, the Spanish and French, and Native Americans, but most of them were relatively brief and confined to a local area. The French and Indian War, which took place from 1754 to 1763, was the biggest war to be fought on U.S. soil until the Revolutionary War. George Washington, who later became the first president of the United States, led Virginia's militia against the French and their Indian allies.

The Shot Heard Round the World

Colonists became dissatisfied with English rule for a variety of reasons. Some reasons were political, some were economic, and some were even personal. However, the first violent conflict between the British and the American colonists was a skirmish over guns and ammunition.

In April 1775, English soldiers marched toward Concord, Massachusetts, aiming to capture arms belonging to the colonial militia. The militia knew of the British plan and had moved the supplies. On the march from Boston to Concord, the redcoats exchanged fire with a group of Massachusetts militiamen at Lexington and scattered them. No one knows who fired the first shot, but it began the Revolutionary War. It became known as "the shot heard round the world."

More Americans were waiting at Concord, and they drove the British back to Boston. The fighting soon spread throughout the colonies. The Minutemen—members of the Massachusetts militia who kept their muskets ready to fight at a minute's notice—would become a symbol of America's fight for liberty.

CHAPTER TWO

TO KEEP AND BEAR ARMS

The U.S. Congress issued the Declaration of Independence in 1776. Americans fought for nearly eight years to make independence from England a reality. During this time, America's national leaders—whom we now call the Founding Fathers—faced important questions. What kind of government would the new country have? Did freedom from England mean that everyone could do as he or she pleased? Everyone agreed that the country needed laws, but who would make the laws? Who would enforce them? How could the people protect their rights? Were there examples of government in other countries that could be copied?

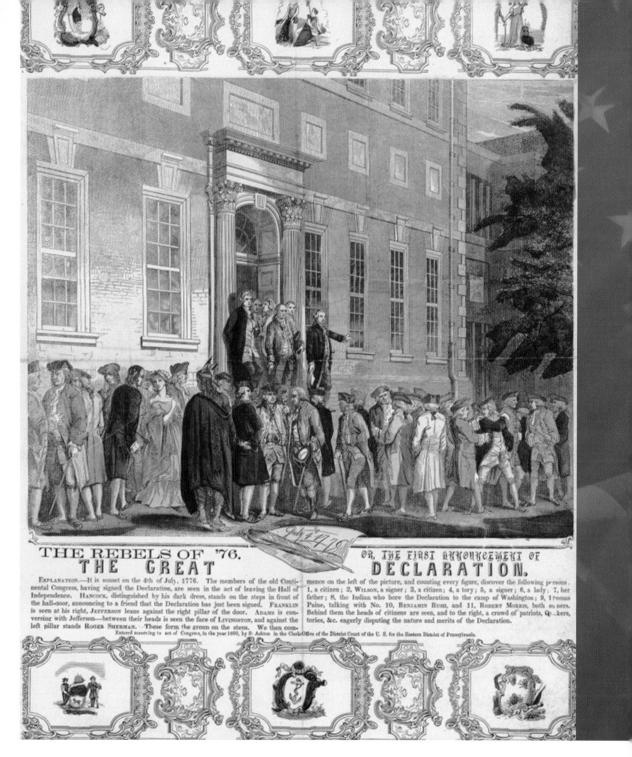

This picture shows the Founding Fathers announcing the signing of the Declaration of Independence outside of Philadelphia's Independence Hall in 1776.

The Militia: Every Citizen Is a Soldier

In the late 1700s, most countries were ruled by kings or nobles. The word of the ruler was law. When the ruler died, power passed to someone in his family. A few people still favored this sort of government, but most of the Founding Fathers had other ideas about how the country could be governed.

They looked back in time to the ancient Greek city of Athens, which had created the world's first democracy. Men who owned property voted on the laws. During times of peace, they worked their farms. During times of war, they fought in a citizen army. A similar system had worked in Rome, although emperors eventually took power. When Rome was a republic governed by citizens, its armies were made up of citizens. However, when Rome was ruled by emperors, its armies were made up of professionals whose only job was to fight.

The Founding Fathers didn't want a king, an emperor, or even a central government with a lot of power. They didn't like the idea of an army controlled by a strong ruler. They remembered how they had been oppressed by England. They had just fought a long and

Fighting during Shays' Rebellion led many Founding Fathers to work for a stronger national government. Under the new Constitution, individual states and the federal government shared control of militia forces.

bloody war against professional English armies. The Founding Fathers decided to let each of the former colonies—now states—make the laws for its people. Each state would be in charge of its own citizen militia.

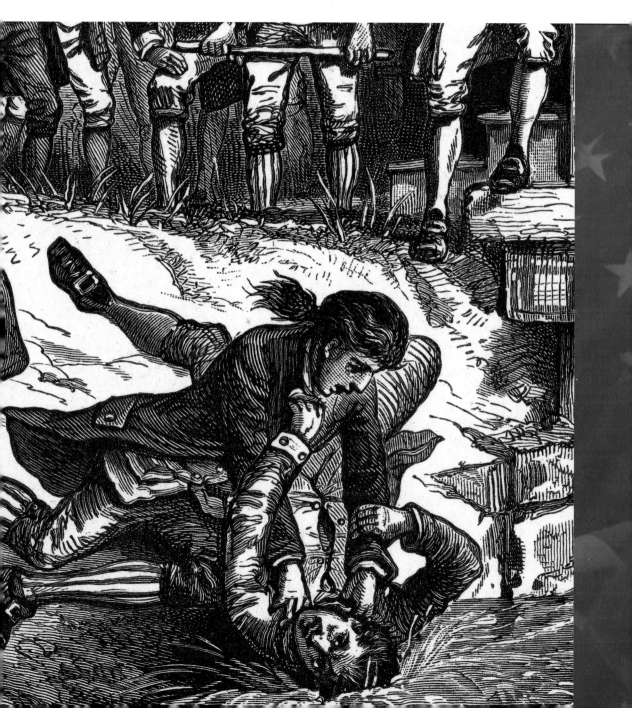

Shays' Rebellion

The first basic laws governing the new United States were known as the Articles of Confederation. Ultimately, they proved to be a failure. After the Revolutionary War, problems arose that couldn't be solved under the Articles. An uprising of armed citizens in Massachusetts focused attention on some of the most severe problems with the new nation's government.

During the war for independence, farmers had left their farms and workers had left their jobs to fight. When they returned home, many of them were in debt. The state governments were in debt, too, because they had borrowed money to pay the costs of fighting the war. Governments raise money by imposing taxes, but at the time, the United States had a weak federal government that had no power to tax. The states imposed taxes, but many people were unable to pay. In western Massachusetts, small farmers owed money to wealthy businessmen in Boston and tax money to the state. When they failed to pay, state courts took away their property.

People fed up with such treatment took out their muskets and began forming their own militia groups. Many of them were veterans of the Revolutionary War who hadn't been paid as promised for their service. One of them was Daniel Shays, who had been a farmworker before the war.

In 1786 and 1787, Shays and others led an uprising against the state courts to prevent them from seizing property and sending people to prison for debt. Local people supported Shays' uprising, but there was little real fighting. When the rebels tried to seize an arsenal full of weapons at Springfield, a state militia sent from Boston drove them away. The rebellion ended soon afterward.

Militias and the War of 1812

As the Revolutionary War began, American leaders soon realized that the state militias could not win independence by themselves. Most militiamen had jobs, farms, and families that they did not want to leave. As a result, they were reluctant to go far from home on long campaigns. Representatives to the Continental Congress created a permanent army in 1775. George Washington was put in charge of both the Continental Army and the state militia forces. He complained that the militiamen weren't always reliable and suggested keeping the army together after the war. Congress refused. The Continental Army was disbanded. National defense would mainly be the job of the militias.

That approach ran into trouble in 1812 when war again broke out between the United States and England. Many militias were poorly led and didn't have equipment. The New England states refused to put their militias under federal control. The English army defeated militia forces outside Washington, D.C. After capturing the nation's capital, the English army burned down the White House and several other important buildings.

The War of 1812 ended in a stalemate, but it was a turning point for the U.S. Army. Many national leaders realized that citizen militias weren't enough for defense. The army was reduced in size but not disbanded. Many veterans stayed in the army to train new soldiers and pass their experience on to future officers.

Americans everywhere were alarmed by Shays' Rebellion and the problems that caused it. The nation's leaders realized that something had to be done.

Federalism and a New Constitution

In 1787, all states except Rhode Island sent delegates to Philadelphia to discuss the country's government. The Articles of Confederation clearly

This monument to the Minutemen is in Lexington, Massachusetts. The Minutemen, who kept their muskets ready to fight at a minute's notice, became a symbol of American freedom.

weren't working. Some delegates to the Constitutional Convention thought it would be enough to make some changes to the Articles of Confederation. Others wanted to throw out the Articles and start over with a new plan.

After months of writing and debate, the delegates approved the Constitution that still governs the United States. It called for a legislature—a Senate and House of Representatives—to make laws; established an executive branch headed by the president to enforce the laws; and set up a system of federal courts to interpret the laws and sort out legal disagreements. The new Constitution divided control of the militias between the states and the federal government. Each state was responsible for training its militia and appointing its officers. However, the president would be able to call out the militias in an emergency.

Before the new Constitution could take effect, it had to be ratified by nine of the thirteen states. Arguments in the state assemblies were often bitter. Those who favored the Constitution and its new federal government were called Federalists. They included Alexander Hamilton of New York and James Madison of Virginia, the main writer of the Constitution.

Their opponents worried that the Constitution gave too much power to the federal government. Samuel Adams of Massachusetts and the Virginians Patrick Henry and George Mason wrote and spoke out for these Anti-Federalists. The Anti-Federalists demanded some guarantees of rights for individual citizens and the states.

At first, Madison didn't think it was necessary to put these guarantees in writing, but in the end, he proposed several of them as amendments to the Constitution. Ten amendments were adopted in 1791 as our Bill of Rights. The Second Amendment said that a "well-regulated militia" was the safeguard of liberty, and that the government could not take away the people's right to "keep and bear arms."

The Founding Fathers and the Second Amendment

Some states had their own bills of rights, which also guaranteed the right to bear arms. Some of them mentioned the right to have guns for self-defense as well as for defense of the state.

The Anti-Federalist George Mason wrote Virginia's Declaration of Rights. One of the items on his list emphasized the importance of a citizen militia and the danger of standing armies, but it didn't say anything about a personal right to have weapons. Much of the language in the Constitution and Bill of Rights is similar to the Virginia Declaration. Pennsylvania's declaration, however, did mention arms for personal as well as militia use. It said: "The people have a right to bear arms for the defense of themselves and the state." Vermont's Constitution said the same thing.

When people during this period debated the right to bear arms, they usually talked about the right to be part of a citizen militia and who would control the militia. Would it be the federal government or state governments? The right to have a gun for hunting or personal defense wasn't a controversial topic, and gun ownership was common.

To Keep and Bear Arms

What exactly does it mean to "keep and bear arms"? These words didn't cause much argument in the 1700s, but they do today. Those who favor gun control today say the phrase had a military meaning for the Founding Fathers. They believe that the word "keep" refers to storing guns in a state armory or other safe place, and "bear" means carrying arms in war as part of an organized militia. This is called the collective right view of the Second Amendment.

TO KEEP AND BEAR ARMS | 25

Those who oppose gun control say the phrase isn't that complicated: it simply means people may also keep guns at home and carry (or bear) them for hunting, self-defense, or any personal reason as long as it's legal. This is called the individual right view.

Although the Second Amendment mentions militias, it doesn't mention hunting, self-defense, or any personal use of firearms. People who want less gun control believe that the individual right to bear arms was so obvious to the Founding Fathers that they didn't see a need to mention it. They point out that many Founding Fathers had their own personal gun collections. People who want stricter gun laws say that if the Founding Fathers had intended to protect personal firearms, they would have said so in the Second Amendment. Some believe the Second Amendment is outdated because most Americans today no longer serve in a citizen militia.

The Whiskey Rebellion

The colonies had agreed that they had a right to take up arms against England. They agreed that people had a right to keep and bear arms. Did that also mean that people had a right to bear arms against their own government?

In 1791, the same year the Bill of Rights was adopted, the federal government put a tax on whiskey to help pay the national debt. Many small farmers depended on sales of whiskey made from their grain. Outraged, they refused to pay. Instead, they protested and harassed tax collectors. In 1794, farmers in western Pennsylvania revolted. The rebels attacked the U.S. mail service, disrupted courts, and threatened to attack the city of Pittsburgh.

Shays' Rebellion had taken place when the United States was governed by the Articles of Confederation. That meant it had been a matter

Pennsylvania farmers rioted and tormented tax collectors during the Whiskey Rebellion. The federal government brought in state militias to end the rebellion, but it let the farmers keep their guns.

for the state of Massachusetts alone. Now the country had a stronger federal government, and President George Washington took advantage of it. He called out the militias of Pennsylvania, Virginia, and other states. An overwhelming force of nearly thirteen thousand marched into western Pennsylvania. The rebels ran and hid. About twenty people were arrested, but there was no real fighting.

The federal government, under its new Constitution, made clear that it would not tolerate rebellion. However, the new Bill of Rights also guaranteed the right to keep and bear arms. The government did not try to take away the farmers' guns.

CHAPTER THREE

GUN CONTROL

s the United States grew in the 1800s, important changes occurred in the way people thought about guns. There were also drastic changes in the way guns were manufactured and in the way guns themselves operated.

Until this time, guns were made by hand. It took years of practice and training to become a gunsmith. Craftsmen would carefully shape each piece so that it fit with other parts of the firearm. If one piece of a handcrafted weapon broke or wore out, it was almost impossible to make a replacement part exactly like the old one. The weapon became useless.

Inventor Eli Whitney created a method for making muskets with identical parts. His system of interchangeable parts led to great improvements in guns and other mechanical devices.

In the late 1700s, American inventor Eli Whitney heard of a French experiment in making identical parts. Workers using the new method didn't have to spend years learning the skills needed to make an entire musket. They could quickly learn how to make just one part—a trigger, for example—and simply make that part over and over. At the end of the process, all the parts would be assembled. If one part was to break later on, the user could replace it with an identical one.

The system of interchangeable parts led to a boom in American manufacturing. New factories were built and workers flocked to towns in the Connecticut River Valley of New England. More rifles and pistols were produced faster than ever before. America became a supplier of guns to other countries. The new guns were cheaper than the old hand-made type, and inventors kept finding ways to improve them.

In 1836, inventor Samuel Colt got a patent for the first revolver. Before this time, pistols had to be loaded like muskets by shoving powder and ball down the barrel. Most of them would fire only once before they had to be loaded again. Colt's pistol had a new type of firing mechanism and a revolving cylinder to hold the loads. It could fire five or six times before reloading.

There were plenty of buyers for the new, improved guns. The country was growing rapidly. More and more people were moving west. In 1803, the United States doubled its size by acquiring the huge territory of Louisiana from France in a transaction known as the Louisiana Purchase. Over the years, settlers moved into the new territory, taking their guns with them.

Early Gun Control Laws

The first gun control laws similar to the ones today appeared in the years between the Revolutionary War and the Civil War. As cities got bigger, people found themselves living closer together. Some began to feel a need for stronger regulations on firearms.

Many places already had laws against the unsafe use of firearms. In Philadelphia, New York, and Boston, it was illegal to shoot inside the city limits where someone could be hurt or killed. In rural North Carolina, it was illegal to hunt after dark. But these laws didn't restrict the ownership or sale of guns.

We have already seen that some of the earliest gun control laws in America were intended to keep Native Americans and slaves from getting arms. The southern states also had severe laws against gun ownership by free black people. Slave owners feared that their slaves would see the example of armed free black people and get their own ideas about freedom. There were few disputes over gun control laws for white people until states began forbidding the sale and ownership of weapons that could be concealed.

Concealed Weapons

People who favored the new laws believed that weapons such as pistols and knives weren't protected by the Second Amendment. These weapons weren't used by militias defending the state, but they were used in crimes or in personal

This modern-day historical reenactment depicts the 1804 duel between Founding Father Alexander Hamilton (*right*) and Vice President Aaron Burr (*left*).

fights. Many people felt there was something sneaky and dishonorable about concealed weapons.

In the early 1800s, men sometimes settled their quarrels by dueling. Alexander Hamilton, one of the Founding Fathers, was shot to death in

a pistol duel with Aaron Burr, the vice president. Dueling gradually died out in the northern states, but it continued in the South.

Kentucky's legislature passed a law against concealed weapons, but the Kentucky Supreme Court struck the law down. A man named Bliss was fined $100 for carrying a sword hidden in a cane. He appealed the verdict and pointed to the state constitution, which said: "The right of citizens to bear arms in defense of themselves and the state shall not be questioned."

The Kentucky Supreme Court agreed with Bliss. It said the state could not limit the kind of weapons a citizen could have. The 1822 case, *Bliss v. Commonwealth*, was the first major court ruling over the right to keep and bear arms for personal use.

Tennessee and Georgia also imposed restrictions on concealed weapons and dueling weapons, and those laws were also debated in the state courts. An Arkansas court ruling went even further than the issue of concealed weapons. It said the Second Amendment protected gun rights for militias but not individual people. Those early cases had

The NRA

The National Rifle Association (NRA) was formed in 1871 to promote marksmanship. It is now one of the most influential private organizations in the United States. The NRA opposes laws restricting firearms.

During its first one hundred years, the NRA was mostly a sporting organization. It sponsored shooting competitions and gun safety education. In the 1950s, the NRA also began to promote hunting and published a magazine for hunters. In 1977, it came under new leadership and became a political organization. Its members were told to vote against any candidate who would try to regulate guns. The NRA currently claims more than four million members, and it contributes millions of dollars to political figures who agree with its goals.

differing results, and they are all cited today in debates over the Second Amendment and what it means.

Ideas in Conflict

By the mid-1800s, the United States was torn by arguments over slavery. Most people who wanted to abolish slavery favored peaceful, political means. But John Brown, a white abolitionist from Kansas, thought it would take violence. In 1859, Brown and a small group of followers broke into the federal arsenal at Harpers Ferry, Virginia (now West Virginia). They intended to seize the weapons stored there and lead an uprising to free the slaves. U.S. Army Colonel Robert E. Lee led troops against the raiders and killed or captured most of them. Brown was hanged and became a martyr for the antislavery cause. Lee later became the most famous Confederate general.

Although African Americans had fought in the Revolutionary War, they were mostly excluded from military service after it ended. However, the Union needed soldiers in the Civil War, and black men were finally allowed to enlist. More than 186,000 black men served during the Civil War, and more than 38,000 died.

Just a few days after the war ended, President Abraham Lincoln was shot to death by a Confederate sympathizer. He was the first U.S. president to be assassinated. The murder sparked fresh anger and resentment between Northerners and Southerners. The road to national unity and equality would be long and difficult.

Three constitutional amendments enacted after the Civil War were intended to correct years of slavery and unfairness. The Thirteenth Amendment abolished slavery. The Fourteenth Amendment said that everyone born in the United States was a U.S. citizen. The Fifteenth Amendment said people could not be barred from voting just because of their race.

The militant abolitionist John Brown and his followers broke into the U.S. arsenal at Harpers Ferry in 1859. They were trying to get guns and start a slave uprising. Brown was captured and hanged.

The Fourteenth Amendment became important in debates over gun control. It said that the states could not deny their citizens any rights that were granted in the U.S. Constitution and Bill of Rights, including the right to keep and bear arms. Because of the Fourteenth Amendment, arguments over state, county, and city gun laws could now be taken to federal court, possibly the U.S. Supreme Court.

Out West

Western settlers hunted and built their homes on land that the Native Americans regarded as their own. Armed conflict between Indians and settlers continued in one area or another throughout the 1800s. Various

Guns in American Culture

Guns and violence have been a big part of American entertainment since the mid-1800s. Civil War soldiers loved dime novels, cheaply printed Westerns featuring honorable heroes who rescued beautiful maidens and shot down sneaky villains. In the late 1800s, William F. "Buffalo Bill" Cody toured the country with his circuslike Wild West show. Audiences watched Indians fight the U.S. Cavalry, while sharpshooters like Annie Oakley showed off their skills. Western movies and TV shows featured lawmen, outlaws, cowboys, and fast-draw shootouts—which rarely occurred in real life.

When it comes to gun violence, the old Westerns seem tame compared with today's popular entertainment. Moviemakers like Quentin Tarantino have been criticized for the violent content of their films. Many of today's most popular video games are "shooters," where players gun down enemies. Guns also have long been a favorite subject in popular music. Many people believe that guns and violence in entertainment lead to violence in real life. Whether that's true or not, there's no denying that guns have played a big role in America's popular culture.

laws made it illegal to supply guns to the Indians, but it was easy for traders to evade the laws. When Indian bands agreed to move to reservations and stop fighting, the federal government agreed to give them supplies, including guns for hunting.

The western mountains and plains provided many hiding places for outlaws and others who wanted to get away from debts or personal troubles. Sometimes a territorial sheriff would call on local citizens to form an armed posse and help him track down criminals.

The word "posse" is taken from the Latin phrase *posse comitatus*, meaning "power of the country." It is part of the "hue and cry" tradition in English common law that requires citizens to band together to protect their communities against criminals.

However, some posses had no legal standing. On several occasions, ranchers got together to keep newcomers from settling on lands they claimed. Sometimes they turned their weapons against minorities. These groups often called themselves vigilance committees, or vigilantes.

The guns used in all these conflicts were deadlier than ever before. More efficient rifles and pistols had been developed during the Civil War. Many of them were repeaters, rifles that held several loads and only needed to be cocked between firings. Some of the newest pistols were semiautomatic, which meant that they didn't need to be loaded or cocked between firings. The shooter only had to pull the trigger.

Figures like Wyatt Earp, John Henry "Doc" Holliday, James Butler "Wild Bill" Hickock, Jesse James, William "Billy the Kid" Bonney, and many others became famous as gunfighters. Some were outlaws, some were lawmen, and some were both. Their real stories were quite different from most of the versions we see today in movies and on television. Life in the nineteenth-century West could be dirty and boring. Quarrels

Jesse James poses with three pistols in this photograph from 1864, before he became a famous outlaw.

were settled with clubs, knives, and fists as often as with guns. In 1890, the U.S. Census Bureau announced the "end of the frontier." The days of settlement and the Wild West were over.

In 1881, President James Garfield was killed in Washington, D.C., by a gunman who claimed to be insane. And President William McKinley was shot to death in Buffalo, New York, in 1901. McKinley's assassination was seen as an act of political terrorism. The assassin was an anarchist, violently opposed to big business and government. People began to call for stronger controls on handguns, and several states enacted laws regulating them.

CHAPTER FOUR

THE SECOND AMENDMENT IN CONTEMPORARY AMERICA

For many years, the right to keep and bear arms was accepted by most Americans without much argument. However, about one hundred years ago, America began to change drastically. Trends and events of the modern era have made the Second Amendment a hot topic today. Some of these include the "war on drugs," gang violence, political assassinations, and mass shootings. Developments that took place earlier in the 1900s include political and racial tension, a prohibition on alcohol, and changes to the old militia system.

The Founding Fathers were used to a system in which every able-bodied man was expected to fight in the militia when necessary. With the exception of the Civil War, the early United States kept its regular

army small. State militias provided most of the troops in wartime. Militia commanders were mostly local men.

By the 1900s, most communities in the United States had professional police forces. The National Guard was established with the

Members of the District of Columbia National Guard clean weapons in this 1916 picture. In the early 1900s, National Guard units became the modern version of state militias.

Militia Act of 1903 and the National Defense Act of 1916. Members of the modern National Guard are volunteers. They are reserves for large national armed forces. In wartime, they are under control of the federal government.

Many people who favor gun control today believe those developments have made the Second Amendment outdated. Some even believe that it should be repealed. They argue that militia service was the reason to let everyone keep and bear arms. Since not everyone in the United States is a member of the National Guard or a police force, it is not necessary for everyone to keep and bear arms.

Political Violence, Prohibition, and Gangsters

The 1901 assassination of President William McKinley by an anarchist was just one of many politically motivated shootings and bombings around the world in the early twentieth century. Anarchists and communist groups trying to overthrow political and economic systems were responsible for much of the violence. Waves of new immigrants were coming to America.

American workers were joining unions, sometimes striking for better wages and working conditions. State and local gun laws were passed during this period to keep arms away from radicals, immigrants, and striking union members.

In 1919, the sale of alcohol was banned in the United States. The following twenty-three years are known as the Prohibition Era. Bootleggers, who smuggled and sold illegal alcohol, formed criminal gangs that clashed with police and each other. The gangsters often used sawed-off shotguns and automatic weapons such as the Thompson submachine gun, or Tommy gun, first produced in 1919.

Prohibition ended in 1933, but gangsters were still around. The country was also struggling with the worst economic depression in its history. A new generation of criminals made headlines: John Dillinger, Charles "Pretty Boy" Floyd, Bonnie Parker, and Clyde Barrow were among the most notorious. The National Firearms Act of 1934 was intended to stop the spread of "gangster weapons," including machine guns, sawed-off shotguns, silencers, hand grenades, and disguised weapons such as guns made to look like canes. It was the first federal attempt to regulate weapons nationwide.

Bank robber John Dillinger (*center*) sits handcuffed to a deputy during a trial in 1934. Dillinger was one of the United States' most famous criminals.

Authorities felt that they couldn't simply ban the weapons because of the Second Amendment. So they imposed a tax on them and made it necessary to register a weapon every time it changed hands. The tax was $200, which was a lot of money during the Great Depression. The act

didn't cause much controversy because most people felt that crime was getting out of hand.

The Federal Firearms Act of 1938 was the first national regulation of ordinary firearms. It required gun dealers to get a license for $1 and to register the names and addresses of people they sold guns to. It prohibited selling guns to violent criminals. The National Rifle Association approved the act.

There weren't any major new gun regulations for the next thirty years. America fought in World War II against brutal dictatorships that had disarmed their own people. Thousands of American soldiers who had been trained to use firearms kept guns at home after returning from the war.

A Wave of Assassinations

In 1963, Lee Harvey Oswald assassinated President John F. Kennedy in Dallas, Texas, with a rifle he had ordered in the mail. The following years were a period of violence and unrest. African Americans marched for civil rights, and the country became divided over the Vietnam War. There were riots in several cities. Malcolm X, a Muslim leader who condemned

Tens of thousands of people joined the 1968 funeral procession for civil rights leader Martin Luther King Jr. in Atlanta, Georgia. Assassinations during the 1960s led to stricter gun control laws.

the oppression of African Americans, was killed with a shotgun in 1965. The Black Panthers, formed a year later, pledged to fight if necessary to achieve equality. The group cited the Second Amendment in its 1966 platform and called on African Americans to arm themselves for

self-defense. In 1968, a gunman in Memphis shot and killed civil rights leader Martin Luther King Jr. Soon after, Robert Kennedy, President Kennedy's younger brother, was gunned down in Los Angeles while campaigning to be president.

States and the federal government began a crackdown on guns. The federal Gun Control Act of 1968 created a list of people who were forbidden to have firearms. They included those convicted of serious crimes, drug users, and people legally declared to be mentally incompetent. Gun dealers were ordered to keep more detailed records. Handgun sales across state lines were restricted. Mail-order sale of rifles and shotguns was prohibited.

The U.S. Treasury's Alcohol Tax Unit (ATU) was given responsibility for guns and explosives. It later transformed to the Bureau of Alcohol, Tobacco, Firearms and Explosives (ATF) and became part of the U.S. Justice Department.

Several gun control organizations were founded during this period. Two of them are still active: the Coalition to Stop Gun Violence and the Brady Campaign to Prevent Gun Violence. Both have changed their names over the years. The Brady Campaign is named for Jim Brady, press secretary for President Ronald Reagan, who was seriously wounded when a gunman tried to kill the president in 1981. Twelve years after that shooting, Congress passed the first federal law saying that people who want to buy a firearm must first pass a background check. The check is designed to stop criminals, mentally ill persons, and drug addicts from buying guns.

The NRA fought the "Brady Law," saying it violated Americans' rights under the Second Amendment. The law was revised, but most of its provisions remain in effect. Today, most background checks are conducted online.

One Town Bans Guns, Another Requires Them

In 1981, the Chicago suburb of Morton Grove, Illinois, made history when it passed a law making it illegal to have a handgun. Even though the District of Columbia already had a similar law, it has a federal government instead of a municipal one. This meant that Morton Grove was technically the first U.S. town to ban gun possession.

When other communities enacted bans similar to Morton Grove's, gun rights organizations challenged the bans in court. Still, the laws mostly remained in effect until 2008, when the U.S. Supreme Court ruled that citizens were entitled to keep handguns for their own protection. Morton Grove repealed its law, and other communities began to do the same.

Kennesaw, Georgia, took the opposite approach. When Kennesaw leaders heard of the Morton Grove ban, they passed a law that said every household had to have a gun. The pro-gun law attracted a lot of attention for Kennesaw, a small town outside of Atlanta.

Both towns got even more attention when gun rights groups reported that crime had decreased in Kennesaw, while it had increased in Morton Grove. Despite all the attention, the two cases don't really tell us much about the effect of gun laws on crime. Few people in Morton Grove had guns before its ban was passed. Most people in Kennesaw had guns before its law passed. In addition, gun crimes were never a major problem in either town, before or after the laws.

Concerns About Violent Crime

Violent crime has been a big concern for many Americans since the 1960s. Drug use, particularly by younger Americans, became widespread during the 1960s. President Richard Nixon declared a war on drugs in 1971. Much of the trade in illegal drugs came under the control of urban gangs. As the gangsters of the Prohibition Era had done, many drug gangs bought the most powerful weapons they could find. Street crime and robberies by drug users made some neighborhoods unsafe. Innocent people were killed in drive-by shootings and street shootouts.

Some of the most troubling events of the past fifty years are mass shootings. Mass shootings are frightening because there seems to be no reason for them, and it seems they could happen anywhere. Some of the most shocking attacks have been at schools.

One of the first was in Austin, Texas, in 1966. A troubled twenty-five-year-old male with a rifle climbed to the observation deck of a tower at the University of Texas. He killed sixteen people before being shot to death by police. In 1999, two students carried a rifle, a shotgun, and explosives into Columbine High School near Denver, Colorado. They killed twelve students and a teacher before killing themselves. The Virginia Tech massacre in 2007 was the deadliest shooting by a single gunman in U.S. history. A mentally disturbed student carried out two attacks on the same day on the college campus, killing thirty-two people before committing suicide. Attacks like these have persuaded many Americans to join in the demand for stricter gun control.

Automatic weapons are on display at a Las Vegas, Nevada, gun show. Many people want tougher restrictions on the sale of firearms at gun shows.

Gun Regulation or Gun Ownership?

All of these trends have sharpened arguments over the Second
Amendment. Many people, including crime victims, demand stronger

controls. Many others want to buy guns to protect themselves and their families.

Most states and cities have some sort of gun regulations. Many require a gun buyer to wait a few days before his or her weapon can be picked up. This wait is intended as a "cooling off" period for somebody who might be angry enough to shoot someone. It also allows time for police to do a background check.

Many of the latest gun control efforts are aimed at gun shows. Since the people selling firearms at these shows aren't regular dealers, they can often sell guns on the spot without background checks or waiting periods. Gun control groups want to close this loophole in the firearms laws.

They also question laws in some states and cities that allow people to shoot an intruder who's trying to steal something, even though the intruder may not be threatening anyone's life. These laws are commonly referred to as "make my day" laws. The phrase comes from a line spoken by the Clint Eastwood character "Dirty" Harry Callahan in the 1983 movie *Sudden Impact*.

The NRA and other gun rights groups are not only opposing stronger gun control laws but are also trying to roll back many of the regulations that are now in place. These groups are known as the gun lobby. Lobbies are special-interest groups whose members traditionally talk to senators and congressmen in the lobbies outside of their meeting rooms. Both the gun lobby and the gun control lobby contribute millions of dollars to politicians' campaigns and use their money to fund court cases. The gun lobby is regarded as one of the most powerful lobbies in the country. Many politicians believe they can't be elected without its help.

Throughout history, the U.S. Supreme Court has heard only a few cases involving the Second Amendment. Most of them did not result in clear-cut decisions. For instance, the *District of Columbia v. Heller* verdict was not a complete victory for those who oppose gun control. While the court said that the Second Amendment protects an individual's right to keep and bear arms, it also said that this right wasn't unlimited. Cities, states, and the federal government may place reasonable regulations on guns.

What is a reasonable regulation and what isn't? As soon as the verdict was announced in *District of Columbia v. Heller*, both sides began preparing for court battles in several cities to answer those questions. One of the first and most important of these cases was *McDonald v. Chicago*. A Chicago man challenged his city's strict laws against handguns, saying he wanted to be allowed to keep a pistol for protection from criminals. At the time of this writing, the U.S. Supreme Court had not made a ruling on the case.

Because guns can either threaten or protect us, millions of people have taken one side or the other in the gun debate, and they have strong feelings about the issue. Of all the provisions in the U.S. Constitution and Bill of Rights, none is as controversial today as the Second Amendment.

AMENDMENTS
TO THE U.S. CONSTITUTION

First Amendment (proposed 1789; ratified 1791): Freedom of religion, speech, press, assembly, and petition

Second Amendment (proposed 1789; ratified 1791): Right to bear arms

Third Amendment (proposed 1789; ratified 1791): No quartering of soldiers in private houses in times of peace

Fourth Amendment (proposed 1789; ratified 1791): Interdiction of unreasonable search and seizure; requirement of search warrants

Fifth Amendment (proposed 1789; ratified 1791): Indictments; due process; self-incrimination; double jeopardy; eminent domain

Sixth Amendment (proposed 1789; ratified 1791): Right to a fair and speedy public trial; notice of accusations; confronting one's accuser; subpoenas; right to counsel

Seventh Amendment (proposed 1789; ratified 1791): Right to a trial by jury in civil cases

Eighth Amendment (proposed 1789; ratified 1791): No excessive bail and fines; no cruel or unusual punishment

Ninth Amendment (proposed 1789; ratified 1791): Protection of unenumerated rights (rights inferred from other legal rights but that are not themselves coded or enumerated in written constitution and laws)

Tenth Amendment (proposed 1789; ratified 1791): Limits the power of the federal government

Eleventh Amendment (proposed 1794; ratified 1795): Sovereign immunity (immunity of states from suits brought by out-of-state citizens and foreigners living outside of states' borders)

Twelfth Amendment (proposed 1803; ratified 1804): Revision of presidential election procedures (electoral college)

Thirteenth Amendment (proposed 1865; ratified 1865): Abolition of slavery

Fourteenth Amendment (proposed 1866; ratified 1868): Citizenship; state due process; application of Bill of Rights to states; revision to apportionment of congressional representatives; denies public office to anyone who has rebelled against the United States

Fifteenth Amendment (proposed 1869; ratified 1870): Suffrage no longer restricted by race

Sixteenth Amendment (proposed 1909; ratified 1913): Allows federal income tax

Seventeenth Amendment (proposed 1912; ratified 1913): Direct election to the U.S. Senate by popular vote

Eighteenth Amendment (proposed 1917; ratified 1919): Prohibition of alcohol

Nineteenth Amendment (proposed 1919; ratified 1920): Women's suffrage

Twentieth Amendment (proposed 1932; ratified 1933): Term commencement for Congress (January 3) and president (January 20)

Twenty-first Amendment (proposed 1933; ratified 1933): Repeal of Eighteenth Amendment (Prohibition)

Twenty-second Amendment (proposed 1947; ratified 1951): Limits president to two terms

Twenty-third Amendment (proposed 1960; ratified 1961): Representation of District of Columbia in electoral college

Twenty-fourth Amendment (proposed 1962; ratified 1964): Prohibition of restriction of voting rights due to nonpayment of poll taxes

Twenty-fifth Amendment (proposed 1965; ratified 1967): Presidential succession

Twenty-sixth Amendment (proposed 1971; ratified 1971): Voting age of eighteen

Twenty-seventh Amendment (proposed 1789; ratified 1992): Congressional compensation

Proposed but Unratified Amendments

Congressional Apportionment Amendment (proposed 1789; still technically pending): Apportionment of U.S. representatives

Titles of Nobility Amendment (proposed 1810; still technically pending): Prohibition of titles of nobility

Corwin Amendment (proposed 1861; still technically pending though superseded by Thirteenth Amendment): Preservation of slavery

Child Labor Amendment (proposed 1924; still technically pending): Congressional power to regulate child labor

Equal Rights Amendment (proposed 1972; expired): Prohibition of inequality of men and women

District of Columbia Voting Rights Amendment (proposed 1978; expired): District of Columbia voting rights

GLOSSARY

anarchist Someone who believes government should be abolished.

appeal To ask a higher court to review a decision by a lower court.

assassination The murder of a public figure, usually by a surprise attack.

automatic weapon A firearm that loads itself and keeps firing as long as the shooter holds down the trigger, or until it runs out of ammunition.

collective A group of individuals who act or work together for a common goal.

common law Law that comes from court cases or tradition, rather than from legislation.

dictator A ruler who governs by his or her own will, rather than by law.

federalism A system that divides power between a central government and members or states with limited authority.

individual A single person or thing.

justice In addition to fairness, this term can also refer to a judge. Members of the Supreme Court are justices.

musket A long-barreled gun that is loaded through the muzzle and fired from the shoulder.

prohibition A law that forbids something, such as alcohol or drugs.

radical Someone whose opinions are far from what is considered normal; an extremist.

ratify To approve something or to make something valid.

repeal To cancel or revoke.

rifle A shoulder-fired gun that has grooves cut inside the barrel to make the bullet spin.

semiautomatic weapon A firearm that loads itself and fires each time the shooter pulls the trigger.

FOR MORE INFORMATION

Bill of Rights Institute
200 North Glebe Road, Suite 200
Arlington, VA 22203
(703) 894-1776
Web site: http://www.billofrightsinstitute.org
The Bill of Rights Institute sponsors programs to educate students about the ideas of the Founding Fathers and our basic freedoms.

Brady Campaign to Prevent Gun Violence
1225 Eye Street NW, Suite 1100
Washington, DC 20005
(202) 898-0792
Web site: http://www.bradycampaign.org
The Brady Campaign supports controls on firearms and maintains a Web site with news and statistics that support its aims. The Web site includes a list of movies and books on gun control. The Brady Campaign also sponsors local programs to prevent gun violence.

Coalition for Gun Control
P.O. Box 90062
1488 Queen Street West
Toronto, ON M6K 3K3
Canada
(416) 604-0209
Web site: http://www.guncontrol.ca
The Coalition for Gun Control supports Canada's gun laws and publishes articles and reports about firearms in Canada.

Coalition to Stop Gun Violence
1424 L Street NW, Suite 2-1
Washington, DC 20005
(202) 408-0061
Web site: http://www.csgv.org
The coalition's Web site has videos, articles, blogs, and links to news items that support gun control regulations and laws. It also has links to its members, which include religious groups, student groups, and public health organizations.

Library of Congress
101 Independence Avenue SE
Washington, DC 20540
(202) 707-5000
Web site: http://www.loc.gov
The Library of Congress offers programs and online resources for students, including documents written by the Founding Fathers, pages on the Constitution and Bill of Rights, political cartoons, and copies of original historical papers.

National Firearms Association
P.O. Box 52183
Edmonton, AB T6G 2T5
Canada
(780) 439-1394
Web site: http://www.nfa.ca
The National Firearms Association publishes the *Canadian Firearms Journal* and gives advice on gun safety and changes to Canadian gun laws.

National Rifle Association
11250 Waples Mill Road
Fairfax, VA 22030
(800) 672-3888

Web site: http://www.nra.org

The National Rifle Association supports the right to keep and bear arms and maintains a Web site with news and statistics that support its aims. It sponsors many youth activities, including an Eagle Scout program, marksmanship programs, an essay contest, and gun safety instruction.

Web Sites

Due to the changing nature of Internet links, Rosen Publishing has developed an online list of Web sites related to the subject of this book. This site is updated regularly. Please use this link to access the list:

http://www.rosenlinks.com/ausc/2nd

FOR FURTHER READING

Aronson, Marc. *The Real Revolution: The Global Story of American Independence.* Boston, MA: Houghton Mifflin Harcourt, 2005.

Bond, Douglas. *Guns of Thunder.* Phillipsburg, NJ: P&R Publishing, 2007.

Cheney, Lynne V. *We the People: The Story of Our Constitution.* New York, NY: Simon & Schuster, 2008.

Elish, Dan. *James Madison.* London, England: Marshall Cavendish, 2007.

Fradin, Dennis. *The Bill of Rights.* London, England: Marshall Cavendish, 2008.

Gonzales, Doreen. *A Look at the Second Amendment: To Keep and Bear Arms.* Berkeley Heights, NJ: Enslow, 2007.

Haerens, Margaret. *Gun Violence.* Stamford, CT: Cengage Gale, 2006.

Karr, Justin. *Gun Control.* Stamford, CT: Cengage Gale, 2007.

Lankford, Ronnie D. *Gun Violence.* Stamford, CT: Cengage Gale, 2010.

Massie, Elizabeth. *1776: Son of Liberty: A Novel of the American Revolution.* New York, NY: Tom Doherty Associates, 2007.

Milite, George. *Gun Control.* San Diego, CA: Reference Point Press, 2007.

Paulsen, Gary. *The Legend of Bass Reeves.* New York, NY: Random House, 2006.

Paulsen, Gary. *Woods Runner.* New York, NY: Random House, 2010.

Roleff, Tamara. *Gun Control.* Stamford, CT: Cengage Gale, 2007.

Rosenthal, Beth. *Gun Control.* Stamford, CT: Cengage Gale, 2006.

Sanders, Nancy. *A Dangerous Search: Black Patriots in the American Revolution* (Adventures in History). Auburndale, MA: History Compass, 2010.

Smith, Rich. *Second and Third Amendments: The Right to Security*. Edina, MN: ABDO, 2008.

Sobel, Syl. *The Bill of Rights: Protecting Our Freedom Then and Now*. Hauppauge, NY: Barron, 2008.

Taylor-Butler, Christine. *The Bill of Rights*. Danbury, CT: Children's Press, 2008.

Taylor-Butler, Christine. *The Constitution of the United States*. Danbury, CT: Children's Press, 2008.

Travis, Cathy. *The Constitution Translated for Kids/La Constitución traducida para niños*. Austin, TX: Ovation, 2009.

Young, Mitchell. *Gun Control*. Stamford, CT: Cengage Gale, 2006.

BIBLIOGRAPHY

Bureau of Justice Statistics. "Crimes Committed with Firearms." Retrieved January 3, 2010 (http://bjs.ojp.usdoj.gov/content/glance/guncrime.cfm).

Cornell, Saul. *A Well-Regulated Militia: The Founding Fathers and the Origins of Gun Control in America.* New York, NY: Oxford University Press, 2006.

Cottrol, Robert J. *Gun Control and the Constitution: Sources and Explorations on the Second Amendment.* New York, NY: Garland Publishing, 1994.

Cottrol, Robert J., and Raymond T. Diamond. "'Never Intended to be Applied to the White Population': Firearms Regulation and Racial Disparity: The Redeemed South's Legacy to a National Jurisprudence?" Retrieved December 17, 2009 (http://www.guncite.com/journals/cd-reg.html).

Doherty, Brian. *Gun Control on Trial: Inside the Supreme Court Battle Over the Second Amendment.* Washington, DC: Cato Institute, 2008.

Free Dictionary. "National Firearms Act of 1934." Retrieved December 27, 2009 (http://legal-dictionary.thefreedictionary.com/National+Firearms+Act+of+1934).

Halbrook, Stephen P. *The Founders' Second Amendment: Origins of the Right to Bear Arms.* Chicago, IL: Ivan R. Dee, 2008.

Hawkins, Karen. "After Ruling, U.S. Towns Rush to Repeal Gun Bans." July 30, 2008. Retrieved November 20, 2009 (http://www.law.com/jsp/law/LawArticleFriendly.jsp?id=1202423379911).

Kates, Don B. "The Second Amendment and the Ideology of Self-Protection." Retrieved December 29, 2009 (http://www.guncite.com/journals/2nd-ideo.html).

Keegan, John. *A History of Warfare*. New York, NY: Random House, 1993.

Kentucky Supreme Court. "*Bliss v. Commonwealth.*" Retrieved December 17, 2009 (http://www.guncite.com/court/state/12ky90.html).

Lienhard, John H. "Interchangeable Parts." Retrieved December 3, 2009 (http://www.uh.edu/engines/epi1252.htm).

McNeill, William H. *The Pursuit of Power*. Chicago, IL: University of Chicago Press, 1984.

More, Rosalie. "Dime Novels and Early Westerns." Retrieved December 19, 2009 (http://www.westernauthors.com/Part_IV.htm).

National Guard Bureau. "About the National Guard." Retrieved January 3, 2010 (http://www.ng.mil/About/default.aspx).

National Rifle Association. "A Brief History of the NRA." Retrieved December 19, 2009 (http://www.nrahq.org/history.asp).

Shapiro, Walter. "Repeal the Second Amendment." Salon.com, April 18, 2007. Retrieved December 14, 2009 (http://www.salon.com/opinion/feature/2007/04/18/second_amendment/index.html).

Sommers, Michael A. *Individual Rights and Civic Responsibility: The Right to Bear Arms*. New York, NY: Rosen Publishing Group, 2001.

University of Missouri-Kansas City School of Law. "Exploring Constitutional Conflicts: A Right to Bear Arms?" Retrieved December 18, 2009 (http://www.law.umkc.edu/faculty/projects/ftrials/conlaw/beararms.htm).

Vandercoy, David E. "The History of the Second Amendment." Retrieved December 28, 2009 (http://www.guncite.com/journals/vandhist.html#fn143).

Volokh, Eugene. "Sources on the Second Amendment and the Right to Keep and Bear Arms in State Constitutions." Retrieved December 12, 2009 (http://www.law.ucla.edu/volokh/2amteach/SOURCES.HTM).

INDEX

About the Author

Larry Gerber is a former Associated Press bureau chief and a veteran of the U.S. Army. He has been researching and writing about social issues and current events for more than thirty-five years. Gerber was a teenager when he got his first lessons in gun safety from his father. He owns one firearm: a target rifle that has been in his family for three generations.

Photo Credits

Cover (left) Rick Gershon/Getty Images; cover (right) Jewel Samad/AFP/Getty Images; p. 1 (top) © www.istockphoto.com/Tom Nulens; p. 1 (bottom) © www.istockphoto.com/Lee Pettet; p. 3 © www.istockphoto.com/Nic Taylor; pp. 4–5 Justin Sullivan/Getty Images; p. 8 © Collection of the New York Historical Society/Bridgeman Art Library; pp. 10–11 MPI/Gettty Images; p. 14 Bridgeman Art Library/Getty Images; pp. 17, 34, 37, 40–41 Library of Congress Prints and Photographs Division; pp. 18–19 Hulton Archive/Getty Images; p. 22 Harvey Lloyd/Taxi/Getty Images; p. 26 The New York Public Library/Art Resource, NY; p. 28 Stock Montage/Getty Images; pp. 30–31 Mario Tama/Getty Images; pp. 42–43 American Stock/Getty Images; pp. 44–45 © AP Images; pp.48–49 John Gurzinski/AFP/Getty Images.

Photo Researcher: Amy Feinberg